Intro to Tagalog

Bela Davis

Tagalog

Abdo Kids Junior
is an Imprint of Abdo Kids
abdobooks.com

abdobooks.com

Published by Abdo Kids, a division of ABDO, P.O. Box 398166, Minneapolis, Minnesota 55439.

Printed in the United States of America, North Mankato, Minnesota.

102024

012025

Consultant: Rayne D.

Photo Credits: Getty Images, Shutterstock

Production Contributors: Teddy Borth, Jennie Forsberg, Grace Hansen

Design Contributors: Candice Keimig, Colleen McLaren

Library of Congress Control Number: 2024936631

Publisher's Cataloging-in-Publication Data

Names: Davis, Bela, author.

Title: Intro to Tagalog / by Bela Davis

Description: Minneapolis, Minnesota : Abdo Kids, 2025 | Series: Intro to language set 2 | Includes online resources and index.

Identifiers: ISBN 9798384902874 (lib. bdg.) | ISBN 9798384903574 (ebook) | ISBN 9798384903925 (Read-to-me ebook)

Subjects: LCSH: Informal language learning--Juvenile literature. | Language and languages--Juvenile literature. | Bilingual books--Juvenile literature. | Language acquisition--Juvenile literature.

Classification: DDC 418--dc23

Table of Contents

Intro to Tagalog

A form of Tagalog is spoken in the Philippines. Let's learn some words!

Tagalog (sound guide) English	Kumusta (ku•muh•stah) welcome

Asia
N
W
E
S
Philippines
Australia

Mga Kulay
(ma•nga ku•lay)
the colors
Kahel
(kuh•el)
orange
Puti
(pu•tee)
white
Dilaw
(deelaw)
yellow
Pula
(pu•la)
red

Luntian
(loon•tee•ahn)
green
Lila
(lee•la)
purple
Bughaw
(boog•how)
blue
Itim
(ee•team)
black

Kumusta
(ku•muh•stah)
hello

Paalam
(pa•lum)
goodbye

Magandang umaga
(ma•gan•dahng oom•aga)
good morning

Magandang gabi
(ma•gan•dahng gah•bee)
good night

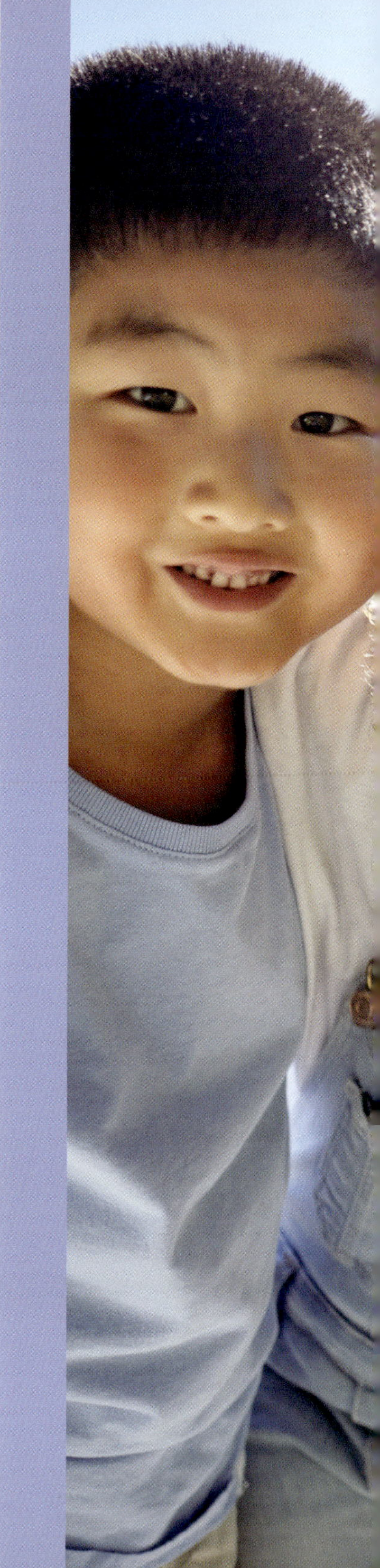

Paki–
(pah•kee)
please

Salamat
(sa•la•maht)
thank you

Oo
(oh)
yes

Hindi
(heen•dee)
no

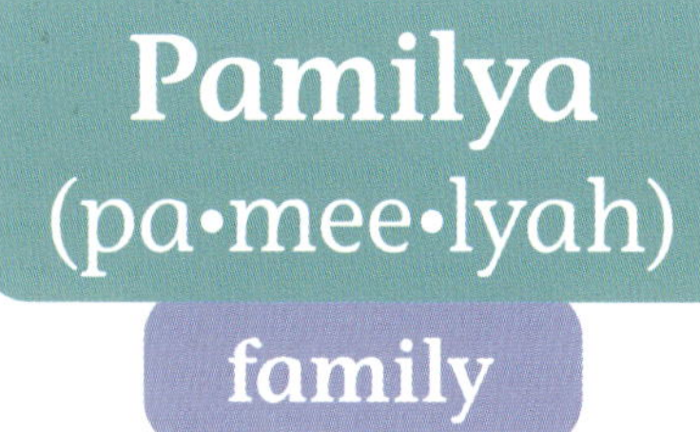

Pamilya
(pa•mee•lyah)
family

Nanay
(na•nay)
mother

Tatay
(ta•tay)
father

Ate
(ah•tay)
older sister

Kuya
(ku•ya)
older brother

Kapatid
(ka•pa•teed)
sibling

bunso
(boon•so)
youngest sibling

Lola
(lo•la)
grandma

Lolo
(lo•lo)
grandpa

Tita
(tee•ta)
aunt

Tito
(tee•to)
uncle

Mga Hayop

(ma•nga hi•yohp)

animals

Ibon

(ee•bohn)

bird

Aso

(ah•so)

dog

Isda
(ees•da)
fish
Pusa
(pu•sa)
cat

Mga Lugar (ma•nga loo•gahr) – Places

Bahay
(ba•hai)
house

Paaralan
(par•ra•lahn)
school

Parke
(par•kay)
park

Tabing-Dagat
(ta•bing-da•gaht)
beach

alpabeto (al•pa•beh•toh) – Alphabet

letter	A	B	C	D	E
sound	ey	bi	see	dee	ee

letter	sound
F	ef
G	gee
H	eyts
I	ay
J	jey
K	kay
L	el
M	em
N	en
Ñ	enye
Ng	engee
O	oh
P	pee
Q	kyu
R	ar
S	es
T	tee
U	yu
V	vee
W	dobolyu
X	eks
Y	why
Z	zee

Index

Visit **abdokids.com** to access crafts, games, videos, and more!

Use Abdo Kids code

IIK2874

or scan this QR code!